Original title:
In the Shade of Coconut Trees

Copyright © 2025 Creative Arts Management OÜ
All rights reserved.

Author: Amelia Montgomery
ISBN HARDBACK: 978-1-80581-620-1
ISBN PAPERBACK: 978-1-80581-147-3
ISBN EBOOK: 978-1-80581-620-1

## Sun-Dappled Dreams

Sandy toes and wobbly chairs,
A seagull steals my crunchy wares.
The sun laughs loud with every ray,
While I chase my drink that rolled away.

Crabs doing dances, oh what a sight,
With their sideways moves, they take flight.
A warm breeze teases my floppy hat,
As I dodge a wayward beach ball—how 'bout that?

## Tropical Tranquility

Coconuts drop, a thump and a roll,
I dodge them like a pro, that's my goal.
Flip-flops flying in the warm, soft air,
Watch out for a rogue frisbee back there!

Sipping juice with a silly straw,
While my buddy builds a castle with 'awe.'
The palm leaves rustle with gossip so loud,
They've seen my most embarrassing moments, I'm cowed!

## Secrets of the Swaying Fronds

Whispers from fronds, a secretive plot,
They're planning to drop coconuts on the spot.
Tropical antics are all around,
With sunburned faces, laughs abound.

Laughter erupts as my chair takes a dive,
The local crabs are all too alive.
"Why's it so slippery?" I gasp with delight,
As a coconut rolls by, oh what a fright!

## Island Hymn of Shadows

Underneath the leaves, I start to doze,
While ants have a party right on my toes.
A shadow looms large, but it's just a cat,
He's got my sunhat, imagine that!

With laughter echoing like waves on the shore,
I'll dance with seaweed and ask for more.
Oh, the joys that the sun brings today,
Now, where did my drink roll away?

## **Lush Solitude Under the Overhead**

Beneath those leaves so wide and lush,
I found a crab with quite a rush.
He danced around, a clumsy feat,
Unbothered by my tasty treat.

With every step, he'd scuttle fast,
No worries for the life he'd passed.
I laughed aloud, what a delight,
His sideways jig, a silly sight.

## Songs of the Fern-Laden Isles

Amidst the fronds with shades of green,
A parrot squawked, a scene obscene.
He mimicked me with all his might,
"Hey there, buddy! What a sight!"

I sang a tune with ample flair,
The parrot chirped, a comical pair.
We harmonized in clumsy glee,
Nature's show, just him and me.

## Enchanted Grove Days

A squirrel planned a picnic grand,
With acorns as his brandy stand.
He spilled his drink, what a blunder,
And chased it down like rolling thunder.

His friends all laughed, it was a scene,
As he turned red, a nutty bean.
They feasted well and shared a laugh,
In nature's joy, they found their path.

## Maritime Melodies

The seashells sang with salty charm,
While fish leaped up, seeking calm.
They plopped back down with a splashy gig,
A watery dance, the ocean's jig.

A crab, quite naive, took a leap,
And hit a wave, oh what a sweep!
With fins and flippers, they'd explore,
The jokes were plenty, laughter galore!

## Secrets Among the Shadows

Under leafy canopies, laughter spills,
Squirrels scurry, plotting little thrills.
A parrot squawks gently, sharing a jest,
Whispers of gossip, secrets unguessed.

The breeze plays tricks, ruffles our hats,
As we chase coconuts, dodging some bats.
Giggling through shadows, we dance and sway,
Who knew palm fronds could lead us astray?

One piglet tiptoes, slips on the sand,
Making a splash — what a clumsy hand!
We burst into chuckles, our sides feel the ache,
Among these tall towers, how much fun we make!

So here we glide, where sunbeams collide,
In giggly delight, let worries subside.
With silly pranks and mischievous flair,
Life is a riddle, laughter's everywhere!

## Sanctuary of Soft Palms

Where the breeze tickles and sunbeams tease,
We lounge like royalty, swaying with ease.
Tropical drinks mixed with laughter so bright,
In this soft paradise, everything feels right.

The hermit crabs shuffle, in a shell on a roll,
While we nap in the nooks, peace filling our soul.
A monkey swings down, steals a piece of pie,
With a cheeky grin, he waves a quick goodbye.

Fish in the lagoon are plotting a dive,
They giggle beneath, oh how they thrive!
While we throw our worries to the playful tide,
Here, in the soft palms, there's nothing to hide.

As shadows grow longer, the laughter rings clear,
Crafting our memories, year after year.
In this playful haven, we cherish and play,
Under whimsical palms, we forever shall stay!

## Beneath the Fragrant Boughs

Swaying leaves above me dance,
A coconut's mischief in a chance.
With every gust, they seem to tease,
Dropping nuts like playful keys.

The seagulls laugh, they see my plight,
As I dodge and weave, a comical sight.
A splat on my head, oh what a treat,
Nature's prankster, oh so sweet.

Sunbathing souls with drinks in hand,
Giggling at the antics so unplanned.
A coconut's grin as it rolls down fast,
Reminds us all, good times can't last.

A pelican dives, aiming for lunch,
Instead he lands, what a silly crunch!
As laughter echoes through the breeze,
Underneath the fragrant trees.

## **Lullabies of the Tropics**

Breezes whisper, tales so sly,
As I nap, they flutter by.
But a furry squirrel, bold and spry,
Decides my snacks are worth a try.

Nuts get tossed and tumbling fall,
A comical scene that beckons all.
With giggles shared beneath the sun,
Our laughter blends, a joyful run.

Beneath the leaves, a hammock swings,
As a breeze plays tunes of silly things.
Falling fruits cause a startled shout,
Who knew a mango could knock you out?

In this paradise of sunny cheer,
Even the shadows seem to sneer.
With a wink from the palms, we feel the vibe,
Lullabies that make our hearts subscribe.

## Beneath the Green Embrace

A soft rustle, oh what a game,
Leaves whisper secrets, oh so tame.
The lizards wink—they're on parade,
While I cackle at their grand charade.

Around my feet, little crabs scuttle,
With quickness and a tiny hustle.
One nips my toe, then makes a dash,
Oh, to be this silly little brash!

Birds sing tunes in a funny tone,
Mocking my dance like I'm all alone.
A flutter here, a flap and swoop,
Turns my flailing into a loop-de-loop.

Sun-kissed moments layered with fun,
In this green embrace, nonsense is spun.
With laughter echoing, we play our parts,
Living life here, full of open hearts.

## Echoes of the Caribbean Sky

Under bright hues, the sky's a blast,
Seashells snicker, what a contrast.
Waves crash loudly, a giggling cheer,
As my beach bag turns into a spear.

A daring crab decides to resist,
Why follow rules? He shakes his fist!
We share our snacks, what a crazy mess,
Nature's comedy is truly the best!

A beach ball lands with a boisterous bump,
Sending sunbathers into a jumble thump.
Oh, what fun, in this sandy spree,
We sing along with coconut glee!

From sunrise bright to sunset's glow,
The echoes of laughter quietly flow.
Every moment, a silly delight,
Under the sky, everything feels right.

## **Palms Dancing with the Wind**

The palms sway with a laugh, and a twist,
As if practicing for a tropical list.
They whisper secrets to the breeze,
While critters strut with utmost ease.

Sun-kissed laughter tugs at the shore,
With crabs on parade, what a sight to adore!
Each wave a chuckle, each splash a cheer,
As clumsy fish take a dive, quite near.

A coconut drops, with a thud and a clunk,
A seagull squawks, feeling quite punk.
The tourists chuckle as they sip their drinks,
While the island plays tricks, oh, what fun it thinks!

As evening falls, they flip-flop and sway,
Under the moon's glow, they dance and play.
Who knew the palms had such rhythm and rhyme?
On this silly stage, we share joyful time!

## Secrets of the Island Refuge

In this land where shadows tease,
A crab wears sandals, it walks with ease.
Parrots gossip, quite loud and bold,
Their tales of travelers, humorous and old.

Bananas giggle as they hang in a tree,
While sunburned tourists sip coconut tea.
A lizard strikes a pose, quite the show,
Winking at folks, as they come and go.

Frogs croak out a tune, oh, such a choir,
As flip-flops squeak, stepping in the mire.
Secrets get traded between breeze and leaf,
In this refuge, we mock our disbelief.

With a wink and a nod, the night creeps in,
The laughter continues, it's a delightful din.
Under a sky sprinkled with stars galore,
Island antics charm us forevermore!

## **Between Leaves and Dreams**

Beneath green boughs, stories unfold,
Tales of mischief and moments bold.
A monkey swings, his grin so wide,
As he snatches snacks, with gleeful pride.

Butterflies flit, all colors and grace,
As they dance around in this playful space.
With every flutter, laughter joins the ride,
While sandcastles watch, bursting with pride.

A hammock sways with a sleepy yawn,
While waves murmur secrets of dusk till dawn.
The dreams of fishermen mingling with fun,
In fabric of laughter, all worries undone.

Between each leaf, a jest waits to bloom,
And underneath this canopy, joy fills the room.
A paradise where silliness reigns supreme,
We share our chuckles, woven in a dream.

## The Cool Caress of Nature

A breeze steals smiles from every soul,
Under the sun's warm and hearty stroll.
With a coconut hat and a cheeky grin,
We dive into laughter, let the fun begin!

The ocean waves giggle as they creep,
While sunbathers snicker and catch some Z's.
Seagulls squawk, what a raucous crowd,
As they steal our snacks, so brazenly loud!

Raindrops tap dance, a lively beat,
While puddles reflect the joyful retreat.
Umbrellas flip, like umbrellas do,
Amidst the chaos, we find our crew.

Nature's embrace, with whispers so sweet,
Encourages folly beneath nimble feet.
With each moment shared, laughter cascades,
Crafting new memories that never fade.

## The Comfort of Coolness

Under leaves so wide and green,
A hammock sways, a comfy scene.
Lizards stare with curious eyes,
While squirrels plot their nutty highs.

With every breeze, a laugh is born,
As my drink spills, I let out a yawn.
The sun tries hard to steal my nap,
But I'm a master of this trap.

Banana peels like slip and slide,
My friends join in, their laughter wide.
Who knew that shade could be so sweet?
In this cool zone, we can't be beat!

## Where Time Slows Under Emerald Canopies

Time ticks slow like molasses drips,
With every sip, a giggle slips.
Birds argue on who sings the best,
While we lounge like we're on a quest.

A coconut falls, a loud thud sounds,
We duck and dodge, laughter abounds.
The breeze teases with hints of sea,
But our mischief is wild and free.

Grass tickles toes, we laugh and play,
Forget the world, it's our holiday.
Caught in dreams, with snacks galore,
Adventure waits just past the door!

## Beneath Fronds of Peace

Under the fronds, we take a seat,
Jokes and stories, all bittersweet.
Sipping drinks with a twist of lime,
Chasing tales that dance through time.

A cat naps near, with a snoozy face,
Stealing warmth and our personal space.
The shadows play tricks, the sun can't win,
As we laugh and let the silliness begin.

There's no hurry, no need to rush,
Just a game of cards and a quiet hush.
With every chuckle, the day melts away,
In the calm of coolness, we choose to stay.

## Shadows of Forgotten Dreams

In twilight's glimmer, fun dreams unfold,
Of adventures eager, yet seldom bold.
A shadow crawls, a chance to play,
With laughter echoing, we drift away.

Forgotten tales of daring deeds,
Are whispered here among the reeds.
As we tease the breeze with silly pranks,
The day dissolves, a carefree flanks.

With every giggle, the night descends,
In shadows soft, where laughter blends.
Time stands still, in joyous streams,
Here's to the fun of forgotten dreams.

## Leafy Umbrellas and Lapping Waves

Under leafy hats, we laugh and play,
Crabs dance about in their comical sway.
The waves join in, giving a soft cheer,
While seagulls gossip, as if they can hear.

With sand in our toes, we leap and we bound,
Finding treasures in shells, what fun can be found!
A coconut falls with a thud and a roll,
We dive for our drinks, what a silly goal!

## **Drifting into Shade and Stillness**

We drift like a boat on the breeze's soft hum,
Spying a squirrel, he's dancing on gum.
While the chatter of waves keeps the rhythm so sweet,
We giggle and toss salty snacks at our feet.

Beneath leafy giants where laughter is bright,
We play hide and seek with the sun and its light.
On this patch of grass, we devise our grand schemes,
Plotting how to catch the stars in our dreams.

## Oasis of Forgotten Stories

In a secret cove where the stories come alive,
We whisper tales where silly myths thrive.
The shells seem to listen, the fish roll their eyes,
While we conjure laughter beneath sunny skies.

A giant dumb crab, king of the beach,
Looks bossy and proud as he struts with a speech.
But we know his secret—a tickle might do,
To send him a-dancing, a joker so true!

## Shade Songs of the Sea Breeze

The breeze sings a tune that tickles the soul,
As we sway with the rhythm, life's sweet little roll.
With laughter like bubbles that flutter and soar,
We sing silly songs, who could ask for more?

The coconuts giggle, caught up in the fun,
As we splash in the surf, under hot golden sun.
With a wink to the sky, we keep the jokes flying,
In this tropical haven, where all are still trying.

## Boughs of Delight

Underneath the leafy crown,
Sandy shoes and beach ball bounce.
Laughter echoes in the breeze,
Crabs dance sideways, what a tease.

Sun hats flip with every gust,
Seagulls eye the chips we trust.
Ice cream drips, a sticky race,
Every lick a happy face.

Tropical fruits, a feast for all,
Pineapple hats, we have a ball.
The playful breeze, a cheeky friend,
Suggests our picnic never end.

Boughs hang low, a playful maze,
In this joy, we lose our ways.
The sun dips low, it's getting late,
But laughter lingers - isn't fate great?

## Visions in the Tropical Haze

Under the palms, dreams take flight,
Silly hats worn with delight.
Mango juice, a sticky treat,
Dance with sand beneath our feet.

Monkeys swing and howl with glee,
Trying to steal our fruity spree.
Sunburned noses, red as a crab,
Smiles all around, we love the jab.

Caught in nets of laughter's hold,
Each silly story grows more bold.
Sunshine paints the day with cheer,
In this haze, we shed a tear.

Even the breeze can't stop the fun,
Chasing shadows from dawn till sun.
Memories made where worries cease,
Echoing joy, a perfect peace.

## **Retreat of the Seaside Fronds**

Fronds dance lightly in the air,
With our toes dug deep, we share.
Salty waves, ticklish and bright,
Splashing giggles in the light.

Napping here, a slapstick sight,
Birds steal snacks in daring flight.
Umbrellas tumbled by a gust,
Who knew that wind could be so just?

Sandcastles towering high, a feat,
Dunes become our royal seat.
Funky sunglasses on our face,
We strut our stuff with utmost grace.

Even the crabs seem to laugh,
At our lopsided, sandy craft.
As shadows stretch and evening grows,
The laughter continues, and joy flows.

## Nature's Shaded Sanctuary

Here we lounge, the world stands still,
Big dreams brewed with fruity thrill.
Foot races held on sandy trails,
Joyful shouts, amusing tales.

Lemonade spills from cups held tight,
Funny faces in the light.
Sunburns painted red as wine,
With every sip, life feels divine.

Swaying chairs and silly games,
Witty jokes, and funny names.
Even a crab joins our fun,
As shadows dance, the day's well done.

The stars peek out, the moon is bright,
Still we laugh through the cool night.
In this sanctuary, we embrace,
Nature's joy, our happy place.

## Embrace of the Green Guardians

Beneath the leafy giants' reach,
The squirrels play their silly speech.
They chatter loud, they leap and glide,
In nature's arms, they take their ride.

A coconut drops with a mighty thud,
It startled me, rolled in the mud.
I laughed so hard, I cried a tear,
A nutty coup, but oh, so dear!

With every rustling leaf above,
I ponder life and what I love.
The lizards dance, all full of flair,
I join the show—who needs a chair?

In this green realm, where fun takes flight,
The guardians grin in morning light.
With every shimmer, smile, and glee,
I'm thankful for this comedy!

## Cool Retreat of the Nature's Canopy

A tiny bug buzzes, quite the pest,
My legs are twitching, they need a rest.
I swat and swish, it takes a dive,
But it returns; it's so alive!

The breeze will tease, it pulls my hair,
I try to look cool, but it's a snare.
It lifts my hat and sends it flying,
A fashion faux pas, there's no denying!

The shadows stretch, the laughter swells,
My friends arrive, with quirky tales.
We roast some snacks beneath the trees,
And ants march in like they own the bees!

The chatter and giggles never cease,
You may find fun, a little peace.
With nature's laughter all around,
In this refuge, joy is found!

## **Rivals of the Rushing Waves**

The ocean roars, it makes a fuss,
While crabs ambush, they don't discuss.
With snapping claws, they dance their game,
I can't help but laugh, it's quite the claim!

Seagulls squawk, they swoop and dive,
Claiming my chips, they seem alive.
I shout, 'Hey! Those are mine!' they don't care,
They wheel and caw, they steal my fare!

A splash of water, a wave surprise,
Soaked to the skin, I can't disguise.
The sea's a prankster, a jokester's best,
But I'll keep laughing, it's quite the jest!

With salt in the air, and skies so blue,
Nature's a comedian, it's true!
In the chaos, I find delight,
As rivals play till the fall of night!

## Mesmerized by the Sway

The trunks stand tall, like silly guards,
They sway gently, with no regards.
I mimic them in a goofy dance,
Twisting and turning, taking a chance.

A parrot caws, oh what a show!
It mocks my moves, puts on a glow.
We form a troupe, a ragged band,
In this feathery, leafy land.

The sun peeks through, in playful beams,
Painting the ground, a world of dreams.
I trip and stumble, a comedy,
The nature's prankster, always free!

With every giggle the wind will share,
We celebrate life, without a care.
It's a circus here, with nature's play—
Mesmerized by the sway, come what may!

## **The Subtle Art of Shade**

A squirrel plots his next heist,
Spying the picnic feast so nice.
Under green skirts, he does peep,
Nuts in his cheeks, he'll not skip sleep.

The sun beats down, it's quite a tease,
While we sip juice, and apps we seize.
He swoops and sways with acrobatic flair,
Crumbs hit the ground, but he doesn't care.

A hammock swings, a perfect plane,
As laughter rings, it's all insane.
Who needs a tan, when shade's the plan?
Just grab a snack, and bask, oh man!

The world's a circus, with wobbly limbs,
As kids giggle and start their whims.
In this refreshing leafy cove,
We play and laugh, we feel alive, we rove.

## **Reverie of Rustling Leaves**

Leaves whisper secrets, playful talks,
While ants march by in neat, small walks.
A crab and seagull play a game,
Who'll get the last fry? Such is fame!

The tree sways gently, a swaying dance,
Revealing nature's little chance.
A coconut drops, and laughter erupts,
Time for the beach, let's not interrupt!

We pace beneath the leafy roof,
Each gust brings giggles, this is the proof.
A coconut swings; it meets the sand,
Blasts of joy, perfectly planned!

In this green realm, we lose all care,
With silly dreams that float in air.
Come share a laugh, take in the scene,
Where nature sings, and spirits glean.

## Between Shadows and Sunlight

The sun's bright rays are never shy,
As shadows stretch like cats that sigh.
A hula girl sways with a twist,
A sunburnt nap; oh, can't resist!

She starts her dance, and everyone stares,
Footloose, on toes, without any cares.
A gust of wind, her skirt takes flight,
Sunblock becomes our day's delight!

Children dart like butterflies,
While the coconut piles reach for the skies.
Hey! That's my drink! The ice has gone,
And here I am, left feeling drawn.

It's a game of wits, the squirrels debated,
As laughter and munchies are all related.
Beneath our leafy roof, we sing,
In shadows and sunlight, we do our thing!

## Dance Among the Trunks

A dance breaks out, with roots and glee,
As trunks hold court, like a grand marquee.
Hands in the air, we move as one,
Clapping to the beat, until we're done.

A worm peeks out, calls it a show,
While crabs join in with a funky flow.
Who knew trees could sway so hard?
Their leafy moves are our backyard card!

A breeze kicks in, and dreams take flight,
As suns get lost in the falling light.
With laughter stirred like a pot of stew,
We twirl and spin, oh, what a view!

In every crevice and grassy nook,
There's joy tucked in, if you just look.
Among the trunks where wild things play,
We dance and laugh the hours away.

## A Dance of Light and Shade

The sun plays tricks upon the sand,
With shadows dancing, hand in hand.
A lizard struts, a comical sight,
While crabs avoid the blinding light.

The breeze hums tunes from far away,
While I try to nap but can't delay.
A coconut falls, it rolls, it spins,
Is it a game? Let the laughter begin!

Beneath the leaves, the whispers tease,
As clumsy seagulls glide with ease.
A flip-flop flies, a splash! A scream!
Who knew a beach could be a meme?

With beach balls bouncing, kids in glee,
I slip on sand - oh, woe is me!
Yet all around, smiles fill the air,
In this sunny circus, we share a glare.

## Echoes of the Coastal Wind

Waves crash softly, whispering tales,
Of sunburnt days and seagulls' wails.
A boat with fish, or so they say,
Got caught in laughter, lost its way.

The tide rolls in like a cheeky cat,
Pulling beach towels, where's my hat?
Children laugh as the water sneaks,
Just like that, it's hide-and-seek!

A crab scuttles, trying to boast,
While beachgoers munch on a snack toast.
I'll share my chips, a noble bribe,
To see more antics from the tribe.

With slick sunscreen and sunglasses on,
We chase the wind till the light is gone.
Funny moments, forever we'll keep,
Echoes of laughter, making us leap.

## Oasis of Calm by the Shore

Where beach umbrellas bend in the breeze,
A lazy dog snores, in perfect ease.
The sun's a joker, playing a game,
While everyone else is hideously tame.

With ice cream drips, and giggles around,
A toddler slips, landing flat on the ground.
A crab waves hi with its tiny claw,
I wave back, near spilling my straw.

Shells gather stories, or so it's claimed,
But this one whispers, 'I'm just sand-named.'
Between chuckles and sighs, we float and sway,
In this serene chaos, we laugh and play.

Cool drinks in hand, toes in the sand,
Life's little mishaps are perfectly planned.
In our beach retreat, we're all utterly free,
Living the punchline that's you and me.

## Surreal Moments Beneath Palm Leaves

Caught in a dream amidst the greens,
A coconut drops; oh! The scene!
Parrots squawk like they own the place,
While I chase shade, a persistent race.

A flip-flop lands, who knows where?
Someone's snack goes flying through air.
The laughter erupts like a cannon's boom,
As sand flies up, echoing our gloom.

Beneath the palms, secrets unfold,
Of sun hats' fates and stories bold.
The ocean waves giggle at jokes,
Where chubby seagulls steal our smokes.

Time twirls like a hula hoop,
We sit and ponder in this goofy group.
In surreal moments, the world's a play,
Where joy's the script and laughter's the way.

## **Reverie Among the Leaves**

Swaying gently, a dance so grand,
A squirrel steals my snack, so planned.
I laugh as he scampers, oh so spry,
While I just sit here, wondering why.

Coconuts drop like bombs from above,
I dodge and weave, but oh, my love!
The shade is cool, but watch your head,
A falling nut can fill you with dread.

Laughter echoes through rustling fronds,
Chasing dreams like an endless bond.
In this leafy world, the fun won't cease,
With nature's chuckles, there's pure peace.

From leaf to leaf, we share a joke,
It's nature's laugh; no need to poke.
Under the canopy, joy is found,
In whimsy's nest, our spirits abound.

## Embracing the Lushness of Life

With each green leaf, a tale unfolds,
Of mischief and fun, a life that holds.
A parrot squawks, the jokes begin,
While I pretend I'm not wearing thin.

Swinging from branches, I spot a bug,
Who thinks it's cool to give me a shrug.
I tip my hat, just don't ask me why,
In this wild party, we're all awry.

Chasing shadows, we giggle and dance,
With creatures leaping as if by chance.
The world spins bright, full of delight,
In this lushness, our spirits take flight.

An unexpected splash from a wayward breeze,
Makes me giggle and fall to my knees.
Embracing the chaos, I'm never alone,
In the laughter of life, I've found my home.

## Whispers Beneath the Palms

Beneath the rustle, secrets play,
As giggles chase the clouds away.
A lizard darts, a comedic scene,
He's plotting mischief, oh so keen.

Sunlight glimmers on the leaf so green,
Where all things dance, a vibrant scene.
A playful breeze tugs my shirt right off,
I join the laughter, and toss a scoff.

Twirling around with arms out wide,
I feel the joy I cannot hide.
With each soft whisper, a chuckle grows,
Among the palms, where laughter flows.

Dancing shadows play peek-a-boo,
While I'm tripping on roots like a fool.
Those whispers linger, a whimsical tune,
As joy erupts beneath the moon.

## Breezes Through the Canopy

The breeze wiggles, a tickle on my nose,
With giggles soaring where sunlight glows.
I trip on roots as I try to race,
But even the trees join my silly chase.

A monkey chuckles, my partner in crime,
As we concoct a joke — it's laughter time!
He swings about, oh what a tease,
And I can't help but laugh with ease.

The sound of rustling brings cheer so bright,
Each twist of the wind is pure delight.
We play tag with shadows, losing track of the day,
In this silly realm, we'll laugh and sway.

A picnic planned but ants stand guard,
The fun's in the chase, oh, isn't life hard?
Before we feast, there's laughter galore,
In breezes that whisper, we always want more.

## Clusters of Calm

Lemonades spill, the sun's too hot,
Flip-flops fly, oh, what a plot!
Napping squirrels in a fuzzy embrace,
Chasing shadows, what a silly race.

Breezes teasing through a lazy day,
Parrots gossip, in their own way.
Sandy toes and sandwiches stray,
Who knew nature could be this play?

A hammock swings, a cat's in tow,
With each swing, it's a comical show.
Sipping drinks that have too much lime,
Laughing off this silly, sunny clime.

Today's agenda? Let's not be wise,
Sunburns are proof of our sunny lies!
With giggles echoing through the trees,
Life's a joke, so just take it, please!

## **A Canopied Reverie**

Under twinkling leaves, we daydream here,
A squirrel's antics bring us cheer.
The ice cream melts on a cheek or two,
Sticky fingers, but who needs glue?

Clouds float by, a parade of fluff,
Each one shaped like a goofy puff.
We share tales of mermaids and knights,
As the sun dips low, we laugh at heights.

Waves crash softly with a wink and grin,
A beach ball bounces under the chin.
Accidental flips, a sandy affair,
Who knew the ocean could be so rare?

As evening creeps, fireflies flick,
We'll catch a breeze, give our hearts a tick.
Together we chuckle, none can miss,
This canopied laugh, a timeless bliss.

## **Palm-Censed Whispers**

The whispers rustle in the coconut crowd,
Mysteries shared, quite loud, quite proud!
A crab in a tux, shuffles nearby,
Bowing politely, oh me, oh my!

Shades of green wave under golden rays,
Each leaf a comedian in playful displays.
Banana peels, a slip and a slide,
Tropical laughter we just can't hide.

Frogs sing backup to the sway of the breeze,
While lizards do their best to tease.
A puddle reflects our silly surprise,
Dunking our toes with laughter in our eyes.

As fireflies dance in this palm-scented night,
We share our secrets, feeling just right.
With giggles and dreams, tomorrow is bright,
In this paradise of whims, we take flight!

## Dance of the Gentle Breezes

Breezes tickle, and off we go,
Chasing butterflies, be warned, don't slow!
A picnic spreads with cakes and jam,
Silly hats, oh, how we scam!

Seagulls squawk their quirky chants,
As we attempt our funny dance.
With crabby crumbles and laughter loud,
We strut and prance, oh, what a crowd!

Sandy castles, they tumble and fall,
A tower of dreams, so small, so tall.
We cheer and laugh at our sandy fate,
Who knew building was so… first-rate?

As stars poke through the evening silk,
We sip sweet cocoa, creamy like milk.
In this festive dance of whimsy and cheer,
Life's funny moments, we hold so dear!

## Chromatic Dance of the Palms

Under the bright sun, they shake with glee,
A frond's twist leading, it's wild and free.
Green and brown laughter, they sway in line,
Dancing to rhythms of coconut wine.

Breezy whispers of tales told before,
Palm leaves sighing, wanting to soar.
In the midst of the fun, the coconuts roll,
Onlookers chuckle, it's a comedic stroll.

Children chime in, with giggles so loud,
Imagining palms are a wacky crowd.
With coconuts laughing, one tumbles down,
The comedic king of this tropical town.

As shadows grow long and the sun starts to fade,
Palms still prance on, in their leafy parade.
For when the night falls, the party's not done,
Under the moon, they'll dance just for fun.

## Beneath the Palm Tree's Gaze

A palm peeks down with a cheeky little grin,
Wondering just who is about to win.
Frisbees in flight, they wobbly glide,
Cracking some shells, no shame in their pride.

Sunbathers laugh as they turn and shout,
"Is that a shadow, or a pirate's route?"
While coconuts tumble, some tumbleweed too,
The palms are cackling, it's all quite a view.

As kids play tag, the palm branches sway,
Gossiping rumors of who'll join the fray.
"Catch that coconut, it's heading your way!"
"This tree is a spy, let's see what they say!"

With evening approaching, the silliness thrives,
A parade of laughs as the moonlight arrives.
The palms give a bow, in a twist and a turn,
While stars join the dance, it's a night to discern.

## Hawaiian Lullaby in Light

At noon, the palms hum a sweet little tune,
Beneath their green arms, we sigh and swoon.
Hula grass dancers prance on the shore,
As shadows throw parties, it's laughter galore.

A seagull swoops down, steals a hot fry,
While a mischievous cat winks with a sigh.
"Hey, that's my lunch!" an elder shouts loud,
While palms giggle softly, forming a cloud.

Tanned tourists tease with their silly sunburns,
While locals complain of the twists and the turns.
Yet under this laughter, sweet whispers of night,
Echo joy and friendship, in soft, glowing light.

As the stars awaken, the palms softly sigh,
Sharing their secrets with the moon in the sky.
Each gentle breeze carries chuckles away,
In the hush that follows, the palms long to play.

## **Palmetto Dreams and Gentle Tides**

Here on the shore, where sea meets the sky,
Palmetto tales twirl, with a wink and a sigh.
When waves come a-callin', they sway in delight,
With mischievous faces, a fluttery sight.

Seagulls parade as the breeze blows around,
While palmettos giggle, making merry sound.
An old flip-flop floats, waving to friends,
And palm fronds lean close, the comedy blends.

The sun dips low, igniting the scene,
With shadows and laughter, quite fit for a queen.
Coconuts rolling, a game begins fast,
A coconut race, oh, this fun can't last!

Stars start to twinkle, the laughter grows bright,
While nighttime's embrace whispers soft and light.
With dreams of the day, the night still trends,
The palms close their eyes, as the laughter transcends.

## Serenity in the Whispering Palms

Under tall fronds, I sit in glee,
A lizard chats, quite cheerily.
The breeze pulls my hat from my head,
And now it's dancing, gone, misled!

My drink, a splash of coconut bliss,
Tipsy seagulls join in the hiss.
They squawk their secrets, full of sass,
While I just admire their dramatic class.

A crab approaches, striking a pose,
I giggle, wondering who he knows.
With sideways steps, he struts with flair,
Claiming this patch, free from despair.

Laughter erupts where shadows sway,
The sun plays tricks, in a merry way.
Life's a circus beneath these leaves,
Where joy multiplies and never leaves.

## **Memory of Sunlit Relaxation**

Lemonade spills on my favorite shirt,
Giggling seagulls, oh what a flirt!
I chase the waves, soft and kind,
While my sandwich takes off, unconfined!

A crab in a race, quite the athlete,
Winks at me, a challenging feat.
The sun winks back, a playful tease,
Matching my laughter with a warm breeze.

My toes dig deep into warm sand,
A fish escapes right out of my hand.
As I laugh at my watery foe,
I realize it's just not my show!

Who needs a towel? This day's divine,
Wet and wild as I sip on brine.
Nature's humor is a grand delight,
Under the sun's soft, glowing light.

## Sun-Dappled Hues of Harmony

Tropical tunes drift on the breeze,
A monkey drops snacks from the trees.
With giggles and sighs, we gather 'round,
While beach balls explode with a funny sound.

Fish in their suits, swimming with flair,
They give me side-eyes, as if to share.
I wave my arms like a noodle gone wild,
As laughter erupts, just like a child.

A splash fight begins, oh what a scene,
Splashes of water, we all feel keen.
With every wave, a chuckle escapes,
Creating memories, where joy often shapes.

A parrot squawks, wearing a grin,
"Come join the fun!" it beckons, a win!
Life's vibrant brushstrokes color our day,
In this whimsical dance, we sway and play.

## **The Tranquil Embrace of Nature**

Beneath bright skies, where troubles flee,
I spot a hermit crab, sipping tea.
He glares at me with a quirky flair,
As if to say, "Why sit, just stare?"

A hammock sways, life's gentle game,
While sand slips through like a playful claim.
I try to relax, but then I roll,
Sprawled on the beach, what a comical stroll!

The sun's a joker, playing with light,
Turning my hair into quite the sight.
With twists and knots that even stars envy,
I can't help but giggle at the absurdity.

In laughter and breeze, my heart feels free,
Among laughter and mirth, I'm meant to be.
This is the rhythm of life at play,
Embracing nature, in a humorous way.

## Shadows of Paradise

Under the leaves where the breezes tease,
Laughter dances, as light plays with ease.
Squirrels on a quest, their acorns they hoard,
While I try my best to balance on board.

A coconut drops with a thud and a sway,
I dodge just in time, oh what a bright day!
Friends gather 'round with a coconut drink,
We clink our shells, making all the trees wink.

The sun liked to laugh, but clouds join the spree,
Sprinkling raindrops like nature's confetti.
We slip and we slide, oh what a delight,
Tripping up roots till we're all out of sight!

But what's that I see? A parrot in flair,
Mimicking my fall, just floating in air.
With giggles and glee, we forget all our woes,
In this goofy paradise, where the fun never slows!

## Murmurs Beneath the Boughs

Whispers of mischief echo through the green,
As monkeys play pranks that are too rarely seen.
Tickling my toes with a leaf in a whirl,
I dodge and I laugh, oh what a wild twirl!

Banana peels scattered, a slip and a slide,
We tumble and roll, with nowhere to hide.
Coconuts chuckle, their shells full of jest,
Nature's own clowns, put our balance to test.

A crab joins the party, all sidestepped and bold,
Thinking he's king, or so I've been told.
With sideways antics, he struts with a grin,
We can't help but giggle at his comical spin.

Under the boughs where the mischief runs wild,
Laughter erupts like a jubilant child.
Gathered in friendship, with joy to expose,
In a realm of greens, where humor just grows!

## Lullabies of the Tropics

Breezes hum softly, a tropical tune,
While crickets perform beneath the bright moon.
A crab plays percussion on sand with delight,
As fireflies twinkle like stars in the night.

Palm fronds sway gently, a lullaby sweet,
As a turtle tiptoes, oh isn't he neat?
With his wobbly waddle, he shuffles in time,
A true island dancer, oh isn't it prime?

And just when you think the fun's at an end,
A sea turtle flips to surprise and pretend.
Against all the odds, he shows off his flair,
With a splashy farewell, that leaves us in air.

So we gather our giggles, our hearts all aglow,
Lullabies in the tropics, where the laughter will flow.
Beneath starlit skies and the moon's silver beams,
We dance through the night, amid whimsical dreams!

## Retreat in the Realm of Greens

We seek a retreat, 'neath the foliage wide,
Where laughter escapes, and worries subside.
A frog plays the piano, in croaks so sublime,
While turtles take turns in their humorous mime.

The breeze tells a joke, but it's lost in translation,
The trees start to chuckle with leafy gestation.
A game of hide-and-seek with a lizard so sly,
He pops out to tease, with a glint in his eye.

One banana peel later, and down goes my friend,
Rolling like thunder, oh where does it end?
Shrieks of delight fill the sunlit expanse,
With each silly stumble, we join in the dance.

So come, join the fun, let the good vibes convene,
In this realm full of greens, where humor's the queen.
Under the canopy where laughter springs free,
We revel and giggle, just happy as can be!

## Floating Thoughts in Tropical Air

A parrot sings with a silly tune,
While I nap under the bright afternoon.
With each snore, a coconut seems to fall,
I hope it lands soft, not on my tall!

Fronds dance like they've lost their way,
I swear they're grooving to a DJ's play.
I wave to a crab who waves back with glee,
Who knew crustaceans could be so free?

The breeze brings whispers of forgotten dreams,
Like fishy tales of laughter and screams.
An island loves to play such tricks,
Turn work into games, not just a fix.

As I sip my drink, a little bird spies,
And steals a sip right before my eyes.
We laugh as he flaps and performs a dance,
Life here's a joke, not just circumstance.

## Eco-Symphony of Swaying Palms

The palms are swaying, oh what a sight,
They groove to the rhythm, morning to night.
Each rustle a giggle, each shake a cheer,
Nature's concert, hold on to your beer!

Squirrels are frolicking, chasing their tails,
On branches above, they spin like flails.
One jumped too far, caught in mid-air,
Lands with a thud, without a care!

The breeze plays tricks, it steals my hat,
And leaves me looking like an old stray cat.
The seagulls laugh, they shout with glee,
"Hey look at the human! Oh woe is thee!"

As shadows flicker, my drink runs dry,
But the laughing fellows never pass by.
We toast to the fun, the nature parade,
An eco-symphony that can't ever fade.

## Nature's Shade-Kissed Retreat

A hammock sways like a ship on the sea,
While I drift along, oh how carefree!
The sun plays tag, it hides and peeks,
To tan me gently, tickling my cheeks.

An iguana slow-walks, with sass and flair,
Like it owns the place, without a care.
It stops to pose, as if to say,
"Take my picture, I'm here to stay!"

Clouds drift lazily, they're chewing gum,
Spitting out rain—but it's hardly a sum!
A tropical shower that cools the day,
I dance in my flip-flops, come out to play.

Laughter erupts as I slip on the ground,
But nature's quick laugh is the best kind around.
With shade-kissed moments that never tire,
I sit with a grin, the island's choir.

## Gentle Hush of Island Breezes

A gentle hush whispers through the trees,
Tickling my ears like a warm summer tease.
Thoughts float away on a puffy white cloud,
While I giggle softly, feeling quite proud.

The dogs take a snooze, dreaming of bone,
While tourists debate how to find home.
I join in their chatter, with silly delight,
While a chicken struts by, claiming the right.

Watermelons roll past, tossed by a breeze,
Nature's fruit games bring giggles with ease.
As I chase after, my laughter erupts,
While old folks chuckle, their wisdom corrupts.

The world's a playground, so take off your shoes,
In this quirky oasis, there's nothing to lose.
With a smile on my face and the sun in my hair,
Life's funny jaunt is beyond compare.

# Under the Boughs of Delight

Under broad crowns where coconuts play, \nA crab dances wildly, stealing my tray. \nWith laughter that echoes, we sip sweet punch, \nWhile the breeze tosses chips, it's quite the brunch.

A bird swoops and dips, trying to steal, \nMy sandwich, my fries—what a raw deal! \nWe giggle and squawk, swinging from vines, \nWhile ants march along, forming straight lines.

Sunlight trickles through leaves, a jig of spark, \nA lizard does yoga, with moves that are stark. \nWe stumble and tumble, our games askew, \nIn this canopy circus, we're the main crew.

So under these boughs, let our merry hearts soar, \nWith jellyfish dances and more laughter galore. \nWith every sweet mishap that makes us all bright, \nWe're the kings of this jungle, taking off flight.

## Hidden Havens of Green

Where vines twist and twine around old tree trunks, \nWe hide from the sun, sharing candy and junk. \nA lizard plays tag in this leafy domain, \nWhile we giggle uncontrollably, losing our brains.

The breeze spills secrets through whispering fronds, \nAs my friend yells, 'Watch out!' an acorn responds. \nWe swat at the bugs with our hats held up high, \nWhile one plucky bee just won't let us lie.

With each falling leaf, we count up the scores, \nAnd reminisce moments when we opened doors. \nTo laughter and nature, 'neath this green canopy, \nWe find joy in chaos, feeling wild and free.

As shadows elongate, we know it's time, \nTo leave our retreat, but return in our prime. \nDreaming of mischief in this lushly built scene, \nWhere everybody's welcome in these havens of green.

## Serene Spaces Among the Foliage

In dappled light where the drumming bug hums, \nWe craft a grand plan for banana bread crumbs. \nBut squirrels have stolen our sweet little stash, \nAnd now we're just left with a lingering clash.

Far-off a monkey swings, mocking our plight, \nWith grins made of mischief, what a sheer delight! \nWhile we kick off our shoes, sweet relief in the air, \nIn serene little spaces, we shed all our care.

Caught in our chatter, we blindfolded a friend, \nWho giggles, then volleyed a fruit, oh what a send! \nThe laughter erupts as we dodge the ripe treat, \nIn foliage zipped tight around burgeoning feet.

So here we gather, our worries at bay, \nEmbracing the chaos that life seeks to play. \nWith joy in our hearts, and a knack for the fun, \nWe'll savor these moments till the bright day is done.

## Oasis of Swaying Palms

The palms sway gently, their leaves dance around,  \nAs we strike ridiculous poses, then fall to the ground.  \nWith sunglasses askew and hats wildly blown,  \nWe claim this oasis, it's our party zone!

The locals stare on, amused by our show,  \nWhile we build a grand castle from driftwood and glow.  \nWith laughter contagious, we decorate sand,  \nOur masterpiece rises, an absurd pirate land.

We quench our thirst with some fruit juice so cold,  \nBut a parrot swoops down, pretty bold!  \nIt snatches a sip before we can blink,  \nAs we burst out in laughter, we barely can think.

In this oasis where joy meets the sky,  \nWe'll invent new games, oh my, oh my!  \nWith hearts light as feathers, we cherish the cheer,  \nPainting the world with endless yesteryear.

## Tranquil Tides Beneath the Thatch

Beneath the leaves, the laughter roams,
A crab performs with clumsy gnomes.
The waves insist on splashing quick,
While seagulls squawk, a feathered clique.

A coconut drops, a perfect score,
Hits Uncle Bob, brings out the roar.
We giggle hard, it's all in fun,
As beach balls soar, our hearts are won.

Children chase shadows, sneaky and sly,
While fish plot schemes to flit and fly.
A jellyfish winks with a glimmering grin,
And the sandcastle battles begin again!

In this merry chaos, we twirl and dance,
With sandy shoes and sideways prance.
Life's a party here, wild and free,
Under the sky, just you and me.

## Palm Shadows and Ocean Dreams

Waves giggle softly, a ticklish tease,
While sunburnt shadows sway in the breeze.
A friend's flip-flop flies into the sea,
"Come back, dear shoe!" as we laugh with glee.

Crabs have a meeting, a secret affair,
While seagulls snicker, floating in air.
A dolphin dives with a splashy cheer,
Making the kids squeal, "Come back here!"

Tiki torches dance with funky tunes,
As we attempt our best hula moves.
Sides splitting from laughter, we can't keep straight,
Our dance is a mix of pure, silly fate.

The sun starts to dip, the sky's a show,
Turning the world to a warm, golden glow.
We toast to the moments, wild and absurd,
With coconut drinks, our laughter's heard.

## Silhouettes of Serenity

In silhouettes cast by the setting sun,
We jest and tease, everyone's having fun.
A lawn chair tips, a friend's in a free fall,
And laughter erupts, it echoes through all.

Palm fronds sway like dancers on cue,
While beach goers strike a pose or two.
A starfish winks, eyeing all the fuss,
"We're just here to laugh, there's no need to rush!"

Sand between toes, a sticky delight,
We playtag with shadows till it's night.
A coconut shakes, it gathers its troops,
As monkeys cheer, joining our loops.

With moonlight above, we build a giant mound,
Out of whispering dreams, life spins around.
In this magical spot, we'll forever be,
Strangers and friends, wild and carefree.

## **Vignettes of Island Life**

Picture a parrot with a sassy squawk,
As it joins in, a spotlighted walk.
Flip-flops flapping, a rhythmic beat,
While we chase a sand crab, never admit defeat.

A rogue wave rises, a splash and a shout,
Bob's ice cream cone, now a whipped-out spout!
With giggles galore, he stands in dismay,
As the tide pulls back, it's the end of the day.

Mentor turtles glide with style so smooth,
While kids mimic them, hoping to groove.
Belly flops echo, the challenge is real,
Victory declared with a hearty squeal!

As the sun settles, our tales intertwine,
Creating a tapestry, stories divine.
With sly smiles and friendship, our creatures combine,
In this playful paradise, we're eternally fine.

## Haven of Swirling Leaves

Beneath the green, a rabbit dances,
Hula hoops made out of branches.
Squirrels laugh at my wild moves,
Chasing shadows, making grooves.

A breeze tickles my silly hat,
While insects buzz like they're all that.
Lemonade spills, oh what a sight,
I sip it slow, trying not to bite.

The grass is a patchwork of cheer,
And birds sing loud, they can hear.
A peeling coconut rolls near my feet,
It's a coconut party—now that's a treat!

As friends join in with goofy tunes,
We twirl around like playful loons.
Laughter echoes, a joyful tease,
In this haven of swirling leaves.

## **Swaying Soliloquy**

Oh, the wind whispers my name so sweet,
As I try to dance on my two left feet.
Lizards nod in approval, it seems,
While I lose myself in whimsical dreams.

My picnic spread is an epic mess,
With crumbs as proof of my food excess.
Ants waltz around, they don't care,
They've got a feast that's beyond compare!

A parrot squawks with a cheeky grin,
Suggesting I join in, let's begin!
So off I go, with flair and flare,
Creating a ruckus without a care.

In the midst of this joyous spree,
I wonder if the world can see.
The comedy cast in every sway,
In my own little Swaying Soliloquy.

## **Light and Shadow Dance**

Sunbeams tickle the ground below,
While shadows play hide and seek, you know.
My floppy hat flops with delight,
As I prance around, a goofy sight.

The coconuts gossip up high above,
Sharing secrets with a hint of love.
A chubby raccoon strikes a pose,
He thinks he's a star, oh, how he glows!

My lemonade stand's a vibrant mess,
With drips and spills—what a success!
Each cup a treasure of sweet surprise,
I serve with laughter and gleaming eyes.

As day shifts from bright to twilight's trance,
We sway together in light and shadow dance.
Each giggle a spark, so full of chance,
In this whimsical, carefree expanse.

## **Calypso in the Coolness**

With a ukulele, I strum a tune,
And the breeze sings back, oh, how it swoons!
A crab joins in with a tap of its claw,
Clapping along, it drops its jaw.

Bananas swing from palms up high,
While monkeys yell, "Hey! Give it a try!"
With fruit hats stuck upon their heads,
They shimmy and shake between soft beds.

A picnic blanket flaps in the air,
Laughing loudly as it takes to the rare.
I chase it down with giggles galore,
Who knew playtime could open so many doors?

Calypso vibes in the warm, cool breeze,
Dancing with all, oh, such a tease!
In this magical realm of smiles so sweet,
We twirl and twirl—oh, isn't it neat?

# Dreaming in the Palm's Embrace

A monkey stole my juice today,
I chased him down the beach to play.
He swung so high, forgot my frown,
We shared a laugh, then fell right down.

The sun is hot and oh so bright,
I dream of snacks, a pure delight.
But seagulls swoop, they've got a plan,
My sandwich gone, oh what a sham!

A crab is dancing by my feet,
He's got some moves, it's quite a feat.
He pinches me and scuttles fast,
That prankster waits, I'm having a blast.

Where palm trees sway and breezes tease,
I laugh so hard, I drop my keys.
A game of hide and seek with fate,
In this wild world, I celebrate.

## Shadows on Shimmering Sands

With a towel draped, I look more chic,
But in the sun, I'll soon be sleek.
My ice cream melts down to my toes,
A sticky mess, that's how it goes!

The beach ball flies, I chase it too,
Tripped on a flip-flop, who knew?
But laughter rings and waves collide,
With sandy friends by my side.

A dolphin jumps, right out of dreams,
And I drop my drink, oh how it screams!
But he just smile, flips with glee,
He knows the truth, it's fun, you see.

Sunburnt noses, playful cheers,
Collecting shells with silly sneers.
In this wacky, warm embrace,
We find our joy in this crazy race.

## **Tropical Refuge**

I found a hat, three sizes too big,
Wore it proudly, did a little jig.
The wind took it, laughed with thrill,
With a chase like that, I can't keep still!

A parrot yells what I can't repeat,
Sipping on lemonade, such a treat.
But then my friend, with a grin so wide,
Wants me to dance, in the rising tide!

The beach is hot, the sky so clear,
I spot a crab that seems to sneer.
He's got a rock, and it's quite a sight,
My friend's shoe's next, oh what a fright!

Beneath the palms, our laughter rings,
Sharing stories of silly things.
In this haven, life's simple prize,
We find joy in each other's eyes.

## Mellow Moments in the Breeze

An umbrella fell, I laughed so loud,
My drink's a splash, I'm so unbowed.
The waves roll in, a foamy dance,
I'm a beach bum, caught in a trance.

A sandcastle tall, my royal claim,
But then the tide comes, oh what a shame!
As it washes away, I can't help but grin,
Even the sea wants to join in!

Beachside here, where the sun don't set,
With each joke cracked, I have no regret.
The breeze whispers tales of carefree sights,
We'll make memories, oh, what delights!

With laughter echoing, we host a feast,
Beneath the palms, joy never ceased.
Let's sip our drinks and not a care,
In this funny haven, our hearts laid bare.

www.ingramcontent.com/pod-product-compliance
Lightning Source LLC
Chambersburg PA
CBHW072130070526
44585CB00016B/1616